for the hope of spring

HYBRID POEMS

SHAMAYITA SEN

PUBLISHERS
Calcutta | New Delhi

Hawakal Publishers
33/1/2 K B Sarani, Mall Road, Calcutta 80
70-B/9 Amritpuri, East of Kailash, New Delhi 65

Email info@hawakal.com
Website www.hawakal.com

Cover art by Sudeshna Chatterjee Kumar

Cover designed by Bitan Chakraborty

First edition: December 2020

Copyright 2020 © Shamayita Sen

ISBN: 978-81-948538-6-2

Price: INR 350 | USD 10.99

for Baba

who taught me to savour life
and name the poems

FROM SCRIBBLING NOTES TO PUBLISHING POETRY

I started writing poetry during my college days. After an amateur attempt for a college assignment, I started scribbling notes to self during boring self-study sessions and called them poetry. Much later did I realise that my style and form are Prosaic and Hybrid. The poems in this collection have been composed over a couple of years as an exercise in healing myself post a series of personal losses and misadventures that I leave for you to decipher while reading the pieces. However a large chunk of the collection has been construed during the lockdown. One will surely locate varied instances of the personal and the political merge to form a score.

With quarantine and social distancing being the only mode of self-preservation and saving one's community against COVID-19, it gave me time for the much awaited soul searching. Like many worldwide, I too turned to art and was quick to choose poetry over writing my Ph.D. dissertation chapters. And, I shall forever be grateful to my supervisor, Prof. Anil K. Aneja, for being so kind to me. Sometimes writing has been cathartic, sometimes trauma-inducing, but mostly helpful. When I had composed fifteen poems in a week, I started compiling them and other previously published pieces, deciding to produce the collection as a book. To my relief, soon did fifteen turn to fifty! I approached *Hawakal Publishers* and they were, as always, prompt and keen to offer help.

The collection has been structured into three parts: On Dissent; Grief and Other People; Love, Healing, etc. The poems speak of daily life, longings and idle musings on human existence, the lives we come across everyday, their personal sorrows and political sufferings. Some poems are inspired by certain life experiences of my friends, relatives and colleagues and I shall be ever appreciative of them for allowing me to commemorate those as universal human emotions. The collection also houses a generous amount of such profound emotions as love, hope and belonging. One's cultural and gender identities are crucial to living their busy urban lives—the poems could be a relief read or a shock therapy aiding one's realization of the same. The images are painstakingly collected through cold Delhi metro rides and Kolkata's warmth to classroom discussions and newspaper clippings. They would be a hearty read for most sensitive souls.

Real life human suffering and their manifold effects on the human psyche slip into forming dream images—this plays a pertinent role for the collection. I have often been intrigued by my own mind space and its trail into various scrunched up secrets and forgotten past. Dreams and the human subconscious are spaces of confluence for multiple stray thoughts abruptly tied up to form a meaningful whole. I am hopeful readers will locate lost pieces of their psyche through these poems, thus helping me pass off my personal experiences as collective conscience or universal meaning making.

This is to acknowledge Sumana Roy for taking out time from her busy schedule to write a blurb for this collection. I shall be ever thankful to her. I would also like to convey my gratitude to Muse India's feature: "The Madness of the World," ed. Semeen Ali, WE View's feature: "Sunday," curated by Somrita Urni Ganguly and *Hawakal's* previously published anthologies—*Quesadilla and Other Adventures: Food Poems*, ed. Somrita Urni Ganguly and *HIBISCUS: poems that heal and empower*, ed. Kiriti Sengupta, Anu Majumdar, and Dustin Pickering, for publishing a few pieces that are now a part of this book.

Shamayita Sen
November 2020
Kolkata

CONTENTS

Love, Healing, etc.

ON DISSENT

LANGUAGE BEARS ROOTS

I've written many poems
in a borrowed language,
one that's not
my mother's tongue,
but one that prompts
co-passengers in a crowded metro
to make a pass at me.

And now that I have
learnt whole the English vowels,
I know how to spit out
neither my borrowed life,
nor erase the torture
on my ancestors in
their native land.

Language bears roots,
branching out through
lips and prayers
calling them home.

A WORLD SHATTERING, FAR OFF

Somewhere while your world shatters,
I sit here,
complacent,
gaping at the stars, admiring the deep blue skies of her eyes,
penning down uncharted worries off her knitted eyebrows.
Yet uncomplaining,
yet unstirred by your shattering world.

How easy is it to brush tragedies
under the carpet
as if
they are words
and abuses,
wars and rage
meant to be left unattended
by governments and Lovers,
like lands and lives to be disputed over,
secretly,
desirously,
like mutton on a Tuesday platter,

or exploring erogenous zones on a premarital bed.

How easy has it become
to consider the rift between
your
shattered world and mine
as palpable!

In Love, In Rage

I

If you tell me to love you
I shall gift you a poem.

A poem about a heart break.

I fetch my heart out of my pocket
and throw it
like a stone hurled in a protest.

II

My heart is a stone.
Not one that I've swallowed,
not one that fills my pocket
  to sink me in oceans of sorrow[1],
but one,
to be pelt in rage
to enzyme a revolution.

[1]Reference to Virginia Woolf's suicide.

DREAM

Without proper documentation
of events, know you're
in the middle of a dream,
(or so Lacan began a lecture)

like silencing Partition violence
or rape survivors
is placing them back to a limbo
they fought hard to be relieved of.

Dream is
a moment of confusion
about waking up within deep slumber,
or is a Kafkaesque
trivializing of memory
to a momentary mishap, like

migrant labourers stranded in
cities or run over by trains
transfixed in
their reverie under the sun.

Dreams sometimes also
teleport the dead into life, but then
can death be a dream too?

OUR TIMES

I
One doesn't need a refresher course
on burying the dead:

most Indians immolate the dead.
First the dead man,
then his wife
often on the same pyre[1].
What else must one do with
a surplus woman[2].

So the government
debates on co-morbidities and
relaxes the lockdown
without a fear of the country
turning into an Italy.

And we wait another truckload of the dead.

II
A dog sniffs through fallen dry leaves
hoping to find a piece of meat.

It is neither autumn nor *akaal*.
Muffled in the memory
of a super cyclone[3], the city
bereaves its people and fallen trees.

There are circulars warning:
The flu has marred lives, and yet
from my window I see a child
blowing wishes into a dandelion.
Probably for a safer world.

Before the virus hit the planet, didn't children
raise voices against pollution and racism
and demand peace and gender equality?
Is the dog aware
of this changing world?

[1]practice of Sati
[2]widow
[3]Amphun, 2020

WOMEN

Some days my tongue is a knot,
on another, my hair.

Hair knots are easy to hold,
while dragging her from one
room to another. The husband,
an enraged ball of purple haze,
unwilling to think straight.

Some days I leave my bed
warm, dripping with my child's laughter.
On another, it's a piece of wood I must
renounce. The difference between
love and violence is

a distance from survivors
huddling in snow to the
hovering rescue helicopter
whose random selection leaves a
window too tiny for hope.

SANS COMPANY

I always go to the same restaurant,
try to locate the same vacant
spot to enjoy
the same drink while reading or
watching the same genre. Like

I'm a carpenter perfecting
my art, every nuance exhausted to the T –
like someone from school
exemplified how to live well.
No human knows the feeling
of being attacked mid-flight
(by an eagle[1]). You see, the art of
breaking monotony
is grave unless

it is a bird's nest
destroyed by a stray stone
or a Kashmiri home by a stray bullet.

[1]Eagles attack other birds mid-flight.

LETTERS NOT WRITTEN

You have the soul of a child
toughened by grave stones
of past-life experiences.
Whatever you visualise turns into
poetry: the Sun
an ingredient to an egg drop soup
you want to melt and feed your
nascent self, the moon a sharecropper's
sickle you want to gift to the
brewing revolution. You have
powers untold. Then should you not
prevent the meandering river
from bleeding so profuse?

From Kalinga to Naxalbari and beyond:
every time, children are
pulled into rebellion.
The sun and moon that run for your

poetry lose their charm
and stumble upon
white sheets begging for relief.
So the schools in the cities grudgingly
open their compounds for
the economically weaker section.

I shall stop at this
for moons shall give way to
suns that gobble whole
your childhood
unless it's heavy monsoon
that's worse for sharecroppers
and guerrilla warriors
ambushing government vehicles
with empty vessels and hungry
children to continue their fight
for lost lands and
right to peaceful sleep.

Grief and Other People

JOURNEYING THROUGH

I

She sits up
from a nightmarish long sleep;
needles pricking her soul
to an ultimate shaking grief –

The mounting up of losses:
a repertoire of emotions
a collage stretched across the city sky.

A *jhumka*, a *bindi*:
not enough to hide the tired soul she wears to work.
The cycle of waking up and
falling asleep –
bogging or nagging,
Eliotish or merely staccato,
she wonders.

Scrapes of wall paper.

Rain drops.

Dew drops.

They don't put sign boards declaring the dangers of an
open manhole anymore!

She won't eat the wallpaper scrapes.
She might, though, the toxic raindrops.

Did it rain all night?
She patterns soft mud with her bare foot.

Cuts and fangs:
she wonderously analyse
deeps and oceans:
she practically colours.

Her head is a topsy-turvy
knows neither its path to glory
nor the route of mourning

II

Then she writes
about the patterns of her mind.
The turns it takes
just before a gallop
or a
sharp fall.

A risk,

not knowing the landing.

Rushing past life, traffic, voices,
smells of old songs,
smoke from burnt children.
Cigarettes.
Street food.
City lights.
Bothered
yet unstirred.

III

She decides to
look down from her balcony.
Sees a bike.

Can she own it?
Is it an escape route?

She wonders.

No! Not about the bike.
About the ownership of spaces –
her balcony.

Coffee?

This balcony overlooks neither greens, nor does it dry
the red-blue-black checkered *lungi* she's grown up see-
ing hanging out in the sun. Where is home? Where is
Baba? "Why am I here, alone?"
Coffee?

Coffee being offered a second time.
"Why am I here, alone?"

IV

She turns back to her study.
Table, strewn with papers she isn't seeing for the first time.

A pen.

A poem.

A broken laptop.

The journal with her name etched somewhere in the middle.
The entirety of a Sunday: worn and tired like the acid washed
jeans that she'd tossed over to the person, the cup of whose
palms society categorizes as a dustbin.

SOMETIMES, I LIE DOWN ON MY STOMACH

and listen to my body.
At the beginning of every cycle,
I feel pain emanating from
the centre of the body
spreading through my thighs like wild fire.
One month the right waist harbours it,
on another, the left of the back.

I lay on my stomach, desperate
to keep the pain under control with the
weight and warmth of the body,
lest I pop a pill and rush
to fulfil my capitalist urges at work.

It's a leisure, really, to hear other stories
of pain and not live them:
of painful shoulders and sore breasts,
of laughter and anxious fingers pointed
at the blood on a pretty pink or lemon yellow
adolescent skirt.

Yes, women are garrulous:
we speak of heart burns and period pain.
But what we talk most is about
badly brought up men thrown into
the world to fetch for themselves
who end up hunting women as career.

And what we forget to discuss
in all the ruckus of words and feelings is
the beauty in Love and Poetry.

MEMORIES THAT SOOTHE

Well, not quite.
I'm tired of sleeping on my childhood bed
peering through the mosquito net into the
thumping cold of a moonlit night;
head resting on a pillow tucked into
my see-saw clouds of memory:
a tinkling *Araby*-like silver bracelet
lost in the pond
of a never-ending dream menagerie.

My blood dripping its jaded way
into self-actualization.

Books, Unread

There are these books, stacks of them, like someone has stocked and piled placards and greeting cards, curated with precision and passion over decades as gifts unsent to partners, friends and lost loves. These books have not been dusted for ages, like someone has let moths and spiders and roaches to nestle there, like that someone knows this symbiotic relationship will harm neither the books, nor the insects, like the insects are offered refuge, like they have no other home to build, like if the book owner tears off the cobwebs, she would be as guilty as government officials turning away refugees and migrants off the mainland, like cleaning the bookshelf would be an *adios* leading to the fatal acknowledgement of her lonely life. But what she most frantically desires erasure is the memory of the impending pain that the words when read might cause her. The fiction, as true to her terrifying life, fear her of them paining her through sleepless nights, their doleful images raking up traumatic memories she's buried deep in her psyche.

GRIEF, GERONTOLOGY, ETC

I switch on the lights unto
your twinkling morning eyes.
A table strewn with memories of
Havisham years.
Black-and-white photo frames
of grandparent-like-faces resembling you.
No smoke, no fights, no sunlight
above these table legs of rickety shine.

I understand not if it is
you in those frames or if it is a continued
reverie.

I wear your lips and fingers, and your
gait awaits a newborn on my lap.
Words that reach you with the
velocity of sound, (are we light years apart?)
neither make home in your head, nor
return as unopened envelopes.

I dream of sex.
I dream of you, dead.
I dream: your hand caressing my head.
I know not if dreams signal a blessing
or a rebirth. No school books provide
frantic answers.

You shut your eyes
and my world drops dead.

I'm happy, at least you are saved of the virus[1].

[1] Corona Virus

THE DRIVER

Beating frantic words, mincing guilt driven
thought clouds into a whirlwind
of coffee, as if speed condones off
the act of leaving an ailed bedside
to pursue dreams of wonder that bubble past
non-existent evergreen grasslands.

Effervescent life tales of office drivers
stuck in their hostel rooms
where roaches nibble
on half eaten pizza. I step out, with
bubble wraps in my mouth and
blow out a chunk of my
cheek cells calling out names
that I know not the taste of as they
drip off prayers,

waving a hand to a passerby
who's confused if it is a welcome note
or a request to pass an information

to the man driving a yellow taxi
home. The stew boils a finger paste
of blood and ginger, I mask
the running red into a never-ending sink
of gasps, mood-swings and
cigarette ash. Hope is the surname
of a girl without a father.

A LOVE SONG

My heart's been humming a song
I found on our chat screen –
the words forming a tapestry
on the white of my mind

sometimes creating a village scenery
I've grown up painting:
a boat, a lonely path leading to a house
by the river nobody crosses; and

sometimes shaping into
dark storm clouds
whispering their curse upon
arable lands.

The words have taken liberty
at disarranging themselves
like a seasoned poet complacent of
previous publications
trick young readers to trust

his liaison with words.

I'm worried. I was told words once
uttered lose their value. Yet lyrics
cajole listeners into pit holes
and gaping wounds that remind them
of past lovers and lost lives,
like each word is a hand-picked song
tucked in the hemstitch of your salwar –
each word a reminder of a failed life,
each opening a tiny door in
your head and all you remember
comes rushing
through floodgates. Into light.

THERAPY

Coffee table conversations quickly
shifting from disorderly placed napkins to
discussions on movies and world politics
to grief being a misnomer that can either
clutch you by your throat and demand
immediate documentation like a half baked
strain of thought becoming a poem or
can be swept across floors into a
nightmare quickly replaced by
an involuntary screen memory or can
become a chunk of swiftly flowing debris
underneath a river bridge trafficking
through midnight mournings to hushed
gossips that ration down lives of fellow
sufferers in other conversations over
measured coffee spoons.

IS IT TOO LATE ALREADY?

The distance between your village
and mine is just a wall cross over,
and yet it feels like I've traveled
far-away grasslands and burnt fields
to make you home.
Seasons pass, breeding colours,
bleeding emotions into rice fields.

A child's fore-finger busy in
shadow play churning secrets
from twigs and rose petals suddenly
points towards me, accusative,
for her lost play-mate
who assaulted her
before he took the run.

And it makes my thoughts run wild:
Would her future relationships
be marred 'cause I have
slept with bruises

you've painted on my skin?
Will her memories in this house make her
grow into an anxious young adult?

Is it too late already?

Tell me, have you ever begun
to rape me
but stopped, thinking of her?

BREASTS

Thinning hair at the middle parting
reminds me of other lost flowers of my body.
Bulging breasts, suddenly sullen like
undulated sound waves, all this while
taut with life feasting upon them,
now unnoticeable, vacant like a dilapidated
tree-house no one comes seeking for.
I wonder what secrets have they hidden
that nomad wind haunts them so?

Every morning I wake up with new ailments
that bear upon birds nestling in the hollow
of my heart. They reject the bits of
stale *roti* on offer, the regular morning alaap
my absent-minded granddaughter chests out.
Neither the tree-house nor will she
outlive these birds that make the bark
so merry, and yet I realize a heartbreak
is a heartbreak is a heartbreak. A heartbreak is
why locusts gnaw upon my sullen breasts.

BECOMING

All through my growing years
every time they asked me, I would parrot:
Winter is my favourite season,
Badminton my favourite game...
so much so that I believed it
until a decade ago when I shifted
to Delhi and began complaining of
bone-chilling winters. Only last year
did I finally start playing badminton,
(and I am still terrible at it.) A woman, a young
colleague had committed patiently
to help me learn. Another promised
to teach me to ride a bike. That never happened.
But I don't complain of men here being
available for anything other than
sharing bedsheets. They like it rough,
not knowing how to seek consent, sometimes
missing both verbal and non-verbal cues.
You see, consent can be withdrawn
even in the middle of an act. But all of that
must be fine, 'cause even young women are
often confused while defining 'rape.' No?

POSTPARTUM

The sky breaking
into ashen rain
falls onto the lap of a mother
whose thighs flap open like
a head post an episode of
traumatic release – the kind of mad
no poetry anthology or
Bollywood showcases,
the kind where you begin by
tearing off your hair first
then the wallpaper,
shamelessly baring your teeth,
shattering your phone screen
begging them to listen to
untold feelings – one leading to
another like a staircase unfolding
itself in a dreamscape
where the more you travel
the less you know yourself.

IN MY PALMS

Cups of my palms, the size of
my heart, can seemingly contain a country:
the cradled head of an infant, a *Bharatnatyam mudra*, a
school hymn on imaginary burning lamps, my deepawali diya,
a late lunch of *daal luchi*, a thick hair chunk tied up in a knot
dripping saline water like drops of morning dew and lemon
juice trailing along the ill torn estuaries of *Sundarbans*,
ghats of *Ganges* to the dirt of *Yamuna* spotted from
a cold metro compartment pushing through
everything nature provides and man
harnesses through eternity,
everything except the
warmth of your hand.

CITYSCAPE

Give me a leaf of grass and I'll weave a poem
from it. And you can run it through my neck,
your veins, all the way to my fingernails –
our bodies intertwined like planets from
another universe crisscrossing paths,
making love, yet not colliding.

Or we can hold hands and baptise things
on our way – glass paintings in railway stations,
station masters in cramped up hotel rooms,
flower pots of bonsai, hem stitch of young
but tattered school skirts –
like in love, the city belongs to us,
like in love, I've become the city.

And as if the city in its full glory should
acknowledge the dying art of Love
and I, out of gratitude, must bare my soul
first, then my body, carelessly dropping
an earring in a crowded bus, muffler in a busy street

and appetite in an empty restaurant.

And must you not realise how with age
the innocence of a leaf becomes a
difficult gift, how one unlearns precious life
lessons while walking down dark alleys!

I'm suddenly reminded of a crow
sans its regular cawing
staring into the void of a brewing storm,
shocked further by the void staring back at it.
Does the crow believe in a world order,
the milky way, the universe, this city,
a genome to this master plan of an
omniscient benevolent God?

PHOTO: BLACK-AND-WHITE

Pain
wriggling on the wall
hanging like a photo frame
whitewashed to a slate clean of
memories.

A hand
frantically searching
a pair of glasses in the dark for a
scrunched up face tucked in
an elbow awaiting
the sun.

Desires
entangled in tubes
bloodied in war crawl
back into my womb waiting
to be cut open seeking
rebirth

only to become
another bespectacled
poser for the black-and-white
photo on a whitewashed wall.

PHOBIA

There's something about bridges I've never liked, not 'cause of their elevation, but because they remind me of a dear friend who has vertigo. Crossing one with him once made me feel powerful. He was afraid and I wasn't. And now when I think of it, I feel guilty. Another time, an ex-lover told me how one childhood night in utter darkness their family crossed a dilapidated bridge in a jeep. The next morning the driver freaked out thinking of their luck. Can you imagine sitting through this story without an ounce of empathy like it is an adventure tale one must pass on as a bedtime story, repeating which must make you feel God-like invincible? Recently I crossed a bridge on foot talking to a garrulous stranger who complained of suffering from vertigo thus needed help crossing over. I'm an introvert. Terrible with small talks. I'm old-fashioned that way. So the walk seemed like a torturous never-ending journey uphill. At once I felt like shouting for help. To stop the walk. Afraid of being kidnapped. Encouraging a stalker. Being intruded upon. For once I felt how it feels to be stuck, encountering one's fear. And it all came crumbling down. My conceit, invincibility, courage. All flattened onto a screen full of frightful faces.

Love, Healing, Etc.

MAA

While shouting out her goodbyes,
Maa cautions the maid,
It's going to rain tomorrow.

I wonder if *Maa* keeps clouds in her *anchol.*

I have my share of discontent.
Her constant nagging triggers
my anxiety. But I tell you:

don't underestimate her concerns.
In their *anchol*, mothers carry
love, spices, safety pins, warmth and raindrops.

And, know:
not all raindrops are muffled sobs.

GHORE PHERA: MY HOMECOMING

I was home this winter vacation.

Kolkata isn't too cold like Delhi or New York is!
Just mild and welcoming enough to peel the afternoon
sun off the oranges,
juiced to perfection for a child's taste buds.

What is home? I asked *Baba* as a child,
I know he was born here, in Kolkata,
but his family comes from Dhaka.
He told me stories of Partition violence that
he had heard from his father,
while he mixed moong dal with fish bones
into his steaming hot plate of rice,
and casually placed a soft little mold of the mixture into
my mouth.
He added,
Home is where the heart is.

While doing PK's M.Phil course on "Long Migration,"
we discussed and debated on the concept of Home.

And while I teach Home as a concept
to young adult minds,
we see struggle and food served on the same page.

In Delhi, while sitting over a plate of mashed potato,
and tenderloin steak,
surrounded by friends, equally home sick,
I crave home in *alu sedho makha-ghee bhaat*.
That is comfort food, soothing my half baked Bengali soul
living a thousand miles away from childhood delicacies of
peas *kachori* and slow cooked
mutton *kosha*.

Despite having lived away from Kolkata for a decade,
the homecoming lunch is what
both *Maa* and I look forward to.
She diligently asks over the phone,
a day prior,
What would you like to have?

And

my mind races from
prawn malai curry to *rabri*,
from mustard hilsa to *mishti doi*,
liquid jaggery,
pitha –
everything that fine dining with friends cannot suffice,
everything that the heart craves for.

And I shout out with excitement:
Anything you wish to cook, Maa!
Anything that would remind me of
my cocooned childhood.

TO MY DEAR GIRLS, WITH LOVE

If your mother while oiling your hair
into parted pony tails cautions you
of male friends and cousins
who might hurt you,
know that she has grown up hearing
similar stories from friends, colleagues
and female guardians,
know that families have long
histories of condoning patriarchal violence.

If your cousin nudges you
and asks you to accompany her to
the ladies room in the middle of
a wedding reception,
know that she is scared to walk
into strange lands alone,
for unscrupulous men lurk in dark corners
making advances that might not be
easy to ward off even in the most
crowded of wedding halls.

If your friend folds a medical parcel
in black polythene and pushes it
in the depths of her bag,
know that she has been mocked and ridiculed
by strangers and over-concerned relatives:
her carefree attitude misconstrued as
careless liberalism.

For stains can be washed
not traumatic memories.

If your friend cautions you from
walking into a busy street,
If your mom enacts to you how to
shield yourself from assaults in busy streets,
If your teacher promises to hear about
your anxious stories of harassment
encountered on busy streets,
know:

it took generations of female silence
for them to speak aloud, and
open their arms to you for
an offer of care, comfort and warmth.

NAINITAL

I

I've visited Nainital with my parents half a decade ago. Now, when I'm here again, alone, it doesn't feel the same.

Baba is not there anymore. Not here, in Nainital, while I feed the fish in the *Tal*, not over the phone, calling up anxiously, all night, concerned about my well-being while I travel away from the lap of Delhi into light and fog.

II

After I'd performed his last rites, my cousin turned my face away from seeing further. We have electric chulas these days, grilling, churning flesh into ash. Science has done a lot: you don't hear the bones of your loved ones crackling while they are on their last journey.

My cousin turned my face away, but the little I saw, I thought, *Baba* moved into light.

III

Nainital has taught me: no matter how well you philoso-phize on and memorialize pain, you are living it through, every time, alone!

Nainital has taught me: *Baba* lives on in every bit of all my life experiences.

Nainital was the last hill station I'd been to with him. And I wonder, if my annual craving for the hills would suffice my daily longing for him.

MUSINGS FROM AN AIRPLANE

I wish I had the intent to write poetry as patiently as I wait for your text all through the day. And let me tell you I would have written you long letters, inviting you to coffee under the sun with neighborhood kids playing around, but I think I'm a bit crazy and I've made you up in my head, not the way Plath had Hughes, but the way I write half-baked articles and dissertation chapters: you, the cloud in my coffee, slurred, dazed, doped in love, en-gaged yet enraged at the slightest provocation, not the way mating animals hoot seeking each other, but the way distant lovers crave redemptive companionship. And, immediately, I wish to run down the aisle of this airplane into your fingers I've never touched, thinking that we'll make love under a warm setting winter sun and I shall feather you with ice, cream and chocolate, but I know, instead of lying on the bed of warm grass, I'll leave: list-lessly, dispassionately, counting childhood anxieties on my fingertips, and instead of thinking that if I touch you, you'll melt, I know I'll rush into believing that certain pieces of intimate information are redundant, and in-stead of inhaling the dew of your skin, I shall peer into a picture that has your supple flesh, a probable bruise, not out of concern, not out of passion, but out of curiosity because acquiring knowledge is a pastime while making love is a sin. And you, the figment of my imagination, know that you are material poets thrive on, and also know that poems that talk about childhood anxieties end abruptly.

IN THE MIDDLE OF A POEM

I think of you,
mid-sentence.
Like a broken spoon,
my tongue still unwilling to let go of
your taste.
And then,

I forget. You become a lost strain of thought.

Mid-sentence, my mind meandering past
another spoon, another meal–
I tell myself:
I've bettered the art of giving up,
consuming whole pieces, not requiring
a fork, a knife, the cold steel of a spoon
to taste delicacies graciously.

You aren't a fish bone stuck in my throat
anymore.

I've mastered the art of eating–
I don't fine dine, neither do I prefer

roadside *dhabas*. I cook. I cook for myself,
exactly the kind of *dal* I like, the fish curry *Maa*
cooked at home. And rice.
The right consistency of each dish.

You don't hurt like a fish bone out of place
anymore.

PERSUASION

Come with me to the sea.
I promise I will not
seduce you out of your asexuality.

Okay, let's at least drink the next time we meet?
That's the closest
we can visit the sea.

(Like I'm a child
holding a conch-shell to my ear
expecting distant sea growls to temper
sea-food cravings.)

LAST EVENING

Your lace bra swings on the
bedstead like a garland of flowers
plucked and placed with patience
to decorate our bed, a grassland beneath
a sickle moon, the perfect accessory to
love-making. Suddenly
the running faucet, a sea beside our
soft brown sand bed, floods the room
and your seashell bra that has survived
many lives unnourished, unhinged,
unplucked, isn't coy anymore.

You and I

fine tune a radio
under a Banyan as old as scriptures
buried under *stupas* excavated from
pre-historic times. Our knees touch sending
telegrams to our nervous systems we know
not how to decrypt. You are busy
solving crossword puzzles, I'm flipping
pages of a novel passed through hands of
pale old library card holders, lost in our tiny
shared earthen pot unaware of decorums
that prevent human relationships
from blooming.

YOU IN MY DREAMS

In my dream
you embrace me from
behind
like all lovers do.
We are so close
that your hand on my bosom
is mine shielding my chest
from an unknown sea of people.
I turn to look at your face
pale against the background
of bedsheets closely
resembling the one
I've admired since birth.
In my sleep
I often meet this face
wearing a motley of bodies
shedding each
like snake skin every
dream.

WAITING

Like the *Krishnachura* tree in its
crimson glory enlightening the neighborhood.
Like the river that circles around my feet,
its clear water helping me pick blue brown pebbles
as if I'm a child again looking for colours in nature.
Like the sweat drenched back of a man
shredding meat into strips of joyous lunch.
Like the soulful laughter of a young boy
wearing a flirtatious charm.
Like the lavender from incense sticks
you lit in evenings to dispel evil spirits.
Like the tinkling of coins that
followed your return home.
Like the lather of shampoo on my hair tired
after a week-long high knots and work ponies.
Like the broken telephone voice
beckoning me home.
Like a breastfeeding newbie tampering with
my nights' sleep triggering postpartum depression.
Like a lost key chain with mangled
steel rings that don't hold keys so well

but is a souvenir from a hill station.
Like a poem half written and abandoned
as a suicide note, misquoted and misplaced.
Like a leaf half eaten by a caterpillar or a
bark perched upon by a woodpecker.
Imagine yourself as one of these
and return. Return to build your home
beside mine. This wait is tiresome.

ON LOVING

A tap on the door
and we release each other from
our embrace as if loving
calls for a secret endeavour
that mustn't turn into stories
lulling toddlers to sleep
for such sleep might infest
sinful dreams of love-making
in their shiny little head.

MISSING

Children playing along the river
like my fingers upon your hair
in a half sunlit room. The cattles
are lowing as I lay beneath
this shade visualising a faraway
corridor flooded with moon light.
The cherry orchard across the river,
a sight to behold, bleeds onto an
evergreen grassland merry hopes
of living together. A pebbled
river bed, too patchy for comfort,
waits patiently for fresh shower every
year like your own two ponies
flying in exuberant ballet at every
occasion that brings itself
home.

RETURNING

Absent-mindedly placed fruits
on the dashboard, moist with glee,
drip juice into a puddle underneath
the wooden tea-table. The puddle fresh
and thick like a pool of blood gashing out
of my glass-shattered wounded arm.
The glass chambers reflect
fleeting moments as I enter the room.
An empty vase stands tall upon the mantle
like an odd reminder of the lighthouse
I walked towards every spring-break,
hand-in-hand with you.

HOUSE-WORK

Smart and whole
but loose on the tongue.

My mother called out:
Do you not remember her at all?
The one who helped you bath
while I painstakingly went to work
soon after birthing you.
Do you not remember anything?

I wait
like spilled milk
yet to be wiped clean off the kitchen floor.
Childhood memories
don't haunt me anymore
except for a few
stray episodes of punishment.
I wait
like a carelessly placed plastic cup
collecting water for no use.

The *pallu* of her *saree*
tightly wound around her waist
to avoid distractions
while sweeping or doing dishes
would be my safe place
to recede into
after school hours.

Baba-Maa came home late from work.
Often later than my bedtime.

POPSICLES

Transparent –
staring into them and
outside into a world,
whole, but
painted pink in blood.
The world inside as well as out –
I am in both places at once
and yet not.

Popsicles,
like magic, churning stories
of a child's glee into grief
like someone has carefully collected
metaphors and life episodes
to write poems previously conceived
as love sonnets but finally dedicated to
children of war or migrant labourers,
wasted, still-born,
robbed of their childhood,
or sometimes even dead.

I must dwell upon this thought, I tell myself
and yet my mind swings
past rough edges to happy memories
of me blowing detergent
bubbles in the tub. I open my eyes
and everything is made picturesque
for future hope and use.

I know not how to contain
either my mind, or this world
with its buckets full
of grievances, lost hopes and bitterness.

MONSOON

I woke up crumbling ochre
leaves layering my bedsheets beside
a window overlooking a street
Mom fell from a rickshaw a
decade back and broke her
left arm. I stared at the silver sun
resting upon a confused haze
of melancholic sky summoning
departed souls and sinful jaded lovers.
It's winter in my heart, it shall
remain so for the three decades
I will have to live without
my father.

Maa tells me stories
of grandpa in cellular jail, his freedom
fighting days, of his lost toe
in an accident as I stare through

the window performing calm amidst
caffeine triggered anxiety. The ochre of
the sheets mellow in surprise.
Winter changes nothing of the dim
streetlights beneath. I pulled an
ex-lover close, desiring a kiss. My uncle
saw it from a balcony above
and complained to *Baba*
who never bothered about
shallow correctitude.

৵

When *Maa* slipped off
the rickshaw I could do little to
rescue her. I dialed a number,
some people came rushing. This country
is community driven–sometimes
helping, sometimes harassing. Only
the street lamp has stayed on,
transfixed, like a loyal lover, droopy
on loveless days. Three decades
have passed by with me staring
outside the window seeking comfort
at sights not offered beyond
the opposite building.

All We Remember

Try recollecting, and all you remember
of life will come in chunks.

You sit waiting, he walks away
in the middle of a conversation
as if the conversation had never begun

or you visit the hills: a sun rising
behind the Kanchenjunga,
as droopy, as silent as the watchers.

Rushing past fragile limbs
that have been taken care of,
patted clean for generations
now stretched upon a stretcher
awaiting medication.

We live in epicyclic circles,
living the same moment in every
lifetime not knowing
the many times we've waited
for that conversation to end,
the sun to rise or this body
to be cleansed and revived.

BARBED-WIRE

I climbed up the stairway to the rooftop
to tell myself an old story about a child
who fled a concentration camp:
thin, limp, weak and hungry, he walked
across a sand stretch to cross a barbed-wire.

I had a suicide note crumpled in
the hollow of my fist. It is a teenager's
who jumped off this rooftop. The note said
nothing about his desires or failures. It was
a sketch of an angry bull with a timid butterfly
above its head. I stayed there for a while

alone, streams salting my sockets.
The story of the child from the camp
and of this neighbour I know not
how to imagine together, only that however
spent and stained, there are lives worth
preserving in the hollow of my palm.

LOVE ME

Like sleep approaches your limbs,
meek and stealthy, or like sprinkled
water droplets on a rain washed
window-pane onlooking rings of smoke
chimneying out of a madman's
bidi, I want you to engulf me. Whole.

No pats on the cheek amidst
a gloom-heavy sleep or the wicked murmur
of my head in deep slumber can drive
passion out of my life. I weave
my hunt around you,
flesh and blood. No rivulet
running gauntlets at my feet
can cajole me out of this desire
of being consumed whole. Love me

like the tired soul that watches
unending waves lapping at the
shore awaiting its home for a
hundredth year. The waves, a calm

of the mother's womb that desire
no rebirth, birthing being a process
continuous in time – of love making,
angst and pain. Love me like this
in continuum.

Or don't love me at all.

BLAND

I always look for the same kind of ending
while seeking inspiration from
poems, fearing a sudden
burst of emotions or an epiphany
hidden somewhere beneath waves
of colours meandering into a
bland yet mouthful and shocking
after-taste. Very few paints

homely kitchen walls, totally bypassing
pungent mention of unpaid labour –
knife slicing through skin cells
mistaken for finely chopped ginger,
sweat dripping off a forehead
covered with cheap fabric.

And those that do, offer an occasional
auditory aid of grinding mortars,
a paste of spices essential in
bringing to life a recipe passed on through
generations of free nurture

and care giving.

Most of what I grew up chewing had
structure, rhythm and rhyme schemes I know not
how to incorporate in my fast paced
fragmented life or feed to
a host of readers whooshing past
similar scarecrow lives.

I came to offer inspiration and comfort
but I guess I have referred to my grandma's recipe
that I suckle on on insipid days of sick leaves.

SELF-PORTRAIT

I

My social media is filled with updates
from students who love me, authors
and contemporaries I admire, friends and
colleagues I've forgotten the smell of –
vanity galore. Find me elsewhere to
understand me. Not there!

II

Unfurl me
not like a teenager playing a red rose
alternating between murmurs of
gratitude and curse,
but like a brûlée
that requires a hard spoon
hammering its way into the soft puddle
of childish delight and crème ganache.

Unfurl me
like a letter returned unacknowledged

unopened, its heaving sighs of
a gift of poetry mistaken for a can of worms.

Unfurl me
like they scalp out layers of skin
to open wombs allowing entry
of a herd of children into this world.

III

Her skin glistens like morning dew
in the summer heat awaiting its due kisses
and intermittent smell of a sweat drenched
muscular back upon her chest, rising and
falling like a musical note, as soft
and delicate as *kalboisakhi* clouds that turn against
the earth, torrential and enraged like
an adolescent unabated in love, unaware
of the desperations and struggles
in the path of a Shakespearean heroine.

IV

My father would often relay,
We come alone, we shall leave alone,
Then why must you be scared of living solo?
I wonder:
had he shared the womb-space,
would he philosophise any different.

If you peer into my mind,
you'll see thoughts floating past
a hollow existence of sort, and yet
I must enact vanity.

Autobiographical much?

My mind is a graveyard where
I bury pieces of terrifying news, heart breaks
and my failed attempts at empathy.

How do you write so well?
A colleague once asked.
I am not overwhelmed by
shallow compliments for poems
already rejected by publishers.

And yet I wonder, *how*?
Probably I dig those graves to string together
memories with metaphors and images
painstakingly collected through
literature lessons over the past decade.

Sometimes under the shower while
scratching my naval clean, I fear
losing these strings of words
into water and blood streaming through

my legs into a drain
clogged with childhood tears, or fear
forgetting them while patting
my supple skin dry only to frantically
winnow the towel for lost pieces.

Sometimes *Baba* would help me
look for suitable titles. But now with
him not around, the black-and-white frame,
not quite resembling the face I fondly remember
does me no good.

Maa is happy I'm writing
while she cooks through her days
of retired life that she had once dreamt of
touring the world with *Baba*.
But I wonder,
is it really a happy thing
to weave poems on finger tips
so relentlessly.
Diving, clenching, digging out
these many untold pieces of grief?
Is writing really cathartic?